PAT DEAN

Fractured Heart and Silent Tears

Mothers Grief, Surviving suicide of her son.

This book was professionally typeset on Reedsy.
Find out more at reedsy.com

Contents

1

Introduction

Nobody would talk about this tough topic for years, let alone write about it. Suicide is something that touches so many lives and is deeply personal to those affected by this tragic event. When I did hear of someone who had passed from suicide, I always thought, "What a horrible thing to have to go through." It never dawned on me that one day I would experience this firsthand. Suicide carries its challenges, dealing with a type of grief like no other. Everyone affected has their own way of coping with their grief there is no right or wrong way to grieve. This is deeply personal to each individual, and they will deal with it, in their way.

Some may find peace in talking about their loved ones and remembering cherished memories, while others may choose to process their grief more privately, often retreating inward. The reactions can be vast, ranging from anger to guilt, and despair in these moments, it is crucial to remember that everyone is on a journey—a journey of healing that is often complicated and challenging to get through. When you, are going through this difficult time, it is vital to recognize that **self-care is key.** Taking care of yourself allows for healing, even though the pain of loss never really disappears.

There are many places where, you can turn for help—offering support, understanding, and community.

- Church: Many find solace in their faith communities, where they can connect with others and receive spiritual guidance.
- Grief Counseling: This will help you get through and help you with your grief.
- Support groups for suicide loss: These groups help survivors connect with others who have experienced similar losses, these can be incredibly helpful. These groups provide a space where you can share your stories and learn from one another who have experienced suicide in their lives.
- Friends and family members: It can help to talk about your loss with others you know.

Other arrangements will need to be sorted:

1. Getting in contact with a funeral home
2. Choosing a casket
3. Arrangements to get the person home
4. Choosing cremation or burial

Find the support you need online, in the phone directory, or even at the hospital to see what is available in your area.

2

Personal Reflections

I am a wife, mother, and survivor of losing a child to suicide, which is a heartbreaking experience that breaks a heart in ways no one should ever have to endure. This loss shakes the very foundations of your family. It is an experience that will linger with me until my last breath—always posing questions in the back of my mind: **why, what if, did I miss the signs?** These thoughts constantly, go through your mind."

This was not like my boy at all; all I could think of was that he must have been in some terrible emotional pain, which was the only explanation I could fathom. Losing a family member in this way is not just a personal loss; it is wide-reaching and affects everyone in the family, their friends, and workmates. Each member of our family and friends grieved differently, facing their sadness differently which was best for them. While some openly shared their feelings, others kept to themselves.

Our boy was someone, who worked hard and would help anyone in need—a much-loved son, brother, grandson, father, friend, and workmate who had recently moved overseas for work. He was starting a new chapter in his life, starting a relationship with a lady he had met online.

This experience has shown me how easy it is not to see things that may be considered warning signs. For too long, mental health issues have lingered in the shadows, stigmatized and misunderstood.

The truth is, that mental illness is often invisible; it can lurk beneath the surface, hidden behind smiles and laughter, making it all the more complex. Now, I believe in the importance of open discussions about mental health, ensuring no one feels isolated or has to shoulder their pain alone.

3

The Call That Changed Our Lives

I was woken early one morning by the telephone ringing—a call I will never forget. Upon answering, I was given the news that would change my life and our family's lives forever: my son had tried to commit suicide and had been rushed to the hospital. To this day, I feel sorry for the family member who had the daunting task of breaking such news to me, especially after she received the information from overseas.

I remember every part of my body aching and screaming out, "NO! This can't be true!" but no sound came out. My heart sank and a deep sense of hopelessness settled over me. Pain—I didn't know what real pain felt like until this moment. I had experienced physical pain, but this was an entirely different entity; emotional pain penetrated my very being and left me feeling raw. I ached in every muscle of my body; my heart felt as if it was physically breaking apart.

Now I had the monumental task of letting my husband and other children know what had happened. Breaking this news was heart-wrenching, but it was only the beginning of an unthinkable journey, after processing what I had just learned and the shock for just a moment,

I knew that the news had to be delivered as soon as possible. The rest of the day drifted slowly as I reached out to the hospital for confirmation and then, we began making arrangements to fly out of the country.

The agonizing wait, for our flight—as there were no available tickets until the next day—felt almost unbearable. I just wanted to be by my boy's side, physically and emotionally present for him. The day was a blur. Two of our children accompanied us, and one stayed home as she was, unable to go. Leaving her behind was difficult, but she looked after things that required attention. For that, I will always be grateful. The hardest part for me was boarding the plane, knowing deep within my heart what I was going to find at the hospital, all the while clinging to a desperate hope that I would be wrong.

4

Arriving At The Hospital

When we arrived at the hospital, I found it hard to breathe my legs felt like jelly as we walked toward the ward. Gripping my husband's hand tightly, I was filled with fear and dread.

When I saw him, I gasped—a heart-wrenching sound escaping me. The shock of seeing my boy attached to so many machines was overwhelming. This was the first and only time we met the woman he had been living with, and I can't describe the emotions that flooded through me at that moment.

I spoke to him, hoping he would recognize my voice and show some sign of life. Seeing his hands move offered us some hope; we thought he would be okay, only to learn that it was merely muscle spasms. A cruel twist of fate was that hope was snatched away so quickly.

At night trying to relax and get some sleep became an impossible task. We wanted to squeeze our eyelids together, which was a hard task. We cried together, clung to one another, and whispered about our cherished memories of him — temporarily allowing us to escape the painful truth. We frequently checked throughout the night for changes, hoping for any improvement.

The doctors conducted tests to assess brain activity, and I found those tests were very hard to witness. All the while, we clung to fleeting hopes that we would hear good news. Sadly, all hope faded, and no positive responses came. The next day, the doctors ran another test— and ultimately, they returned with the devastating news: our boy was brain dead. We had reached the point of no return.

Once a person is pronounced brain dead, the hospital has protocols concerning life support. They will shut off the machines within days unless the family makes, that decision themselves. As the next of kin, I found myself thrust into a role I had never anticipated. I have always thought that children should be laying their parents to rest not the other way around. The weight of that decision felt unbearable, especially as I grappled with my grief and the heartache that surrounded our entire family.

I desperately hoped this would be the last of the bad news, but it was merely the beginning of an even deeper nightmare. Our son had expressed a desire to donate his organs; we communicated this to the hospital staff, understanding how crucial it was to offer life to someone else in his memory. Yet, moments later, the hospital informed us that the woman he had been living with had objected and would not agree to organ donation she even asked the hospital to see if we would allow posthumous sperm retrieval.

Hearing this news shattered us again in ways we didn't think possible; I said no and insisted that the life support machines be switched off. Thinking I was putting an end to what we had been asked. As the hospital had me as next of kin, I couldn't believe what I was hearing but I found that was all I could do. I was dealing with feelings of anger, confusion, and betrayal. We questioned why the hospital was delaying the process; this was not a legal matter of negotiation, but a deeply personal tragedy—the loss of life, of a son, a brother, a father, a grandson, an uncle, and a friend.

After several agonizing hours, we learned the hospital was entangled in discussions with the woman's lawyer. Five hours later, they finally came to turn off the machines. This being the saddest thing as a family, we faced one of the hardest decisions of our lives. Even within the depths of our grief, we held onto the belief that in death, he could have fulfilled a final gift—saving lives something I am sure would have disappointed him knowing it wasn't to be.

5

Ongoing Nightmare

As the sun rose the following day, we felt a sense of hope that maybe things would begin to be clearer. We were called to an appointment with the police—a procedure standard in cases of suicide. They informed us that the woman's lawyer was filing papers to get approval for posthumous sperm retrieval. We felt blindsided, bewildered by this new turn of events.

We were quickly advised to seek legal counsel. After consulting with a lawyer, we learned that if we consented to the retrieval, she (the woman) would allow us to take our boy out of the country taking him home to lay him to rest. Ultimately, we felt we had no option but this decision felt less like a choice and more like a forced condition.

To add to the turmoil, the case had garnered media attention, which further complicated the situation they were getting in contact asking for more information about things related to our boy.

Finally, the day arrived when we were able to get our boy sent home, it was only 7 months earlier he was excited to fly out and start a new chapter in his life. Endless paperwork and legal discussions were still ahead of us.

Even with our boy finally home, we still needed closure—an opportunity to lay him to rest with dignity, against the backdrop of all the turmoil surrounding it. As we gathered to celebrate his life, an overwhelming wave of emotions washed over us. Buried beneath all the sorrow was an incredible amount of love shown for him. Laying him to rest was filled with memories that reminded us of his laughter, his hard work, and his kindness.

6

Time for Closure

Since we had laid our boy to rest it was time to get closure so we could move on, until this was done, we would not find piece. I contacted our lawyer, who informed us, that he didn't think the woman would take this matter further. We still had to wait for final confirmation that this was so. Finally, we got word that this part of our horrible nightmare was finally over.

Now it was time to heal, grief had taken its toll on us all. Yes, we all cuddled and cried together as a family but I hadn't realized how much of a toll it had taken on me. The time came to seek counseling, this is something until you are there and have gone through the process you don't realize how badly you needed extra help getting through everything that we had gone through.

Seeking counseling is something people don't like to admit they need which is a shame these professionals are here to help everyone who needs help, after getting the help and sorting through things I was able to heal. No, I have not got over my loss but I have been able to move on.

I will be forever grateful to all our children, family, and friends who had given us all their love and support through this horrible time I don't think I would have survived without it, I love you all so much.

Coping and accepting the death of our child took time, which is filled with reminders of him in many things—a favorite song, a photograph, movies, or different sayings he would say. I share this because I wanted to give hope to others, who may be in the same position and I also suggest others speak up and combat stigma, with me and let them know that it is okay not to be okay but someday you will be healed.

It has been several years since this tragic event happened; I cherish the good times I had and will always remember him not just for his sad passing, but for the beautiful person he was and he will be forever loved.

Losing your child to suicide breaks your heart in ways no one should ever have to experience. The agony of such a tragic loss crushes you leaving you feeling broken. By sharing my experience, I hoped to bring light to others who may be struggling with similar challenges and I encourage others to reach out for help when required and to remind them that it is okay not to be alright, but over time you will heal.

Here's one of the important points to remember, it is imperative that grieving is not an event, it is not something in the sense of which is not something that can be "solved" or "gotten over." In contrast to cessation of grief wherein people tend to erase their grieving memories, bereavement adjustment affects such memories and moves on without avoiding grief. Listening to this aspect of the experience has given me more insight into the experience, more reconstructed around feelings of love and caring, kindness, mercy, and optimism.

7

Understanding Suicide

Definition: Suicide is an act where someone chooses to take their own life causing himself or herself bodily harm. When this is not successful it is called an attempted suicide. Suicide is something that can involve anyone of any race, or age, whether they are rich or poor. This can cause many problems and can affect individuals, families, and people in their lives. The good news is that suicide is **preventable**.

Statistics: Every year, millions of people all over the world are seriously thinking about suicide, planning, or attempting suicide with over 700,000 people dying each year globally. Suicide affects all age groups, particularly among teens and young adults.

Risk Factors: Many things contribute to suicide.
Mental health issues (Depression, anxiety, bipolar disorder)
Substance abuse
Trauma and abuse history
Social isolation or lack of support
Chronic illness or pain
A major disappointment or loss

Broken up with partner or lost custody of children

Struggling to find work, money problems

Feel they are not being supported by family and friends

Warning Signs:

Talking about wanting to die or feeling hopeless

Increased substance use

Withdrawal from friends and activities

Changes in mood or behavior

Giving away their prize possessions

Being bullied

Cutting themselves

Sleep a lot more or not getting enough sleep

Drinking more alcohol than normal

In this modern age, with all the different websites and platforms it is a good idea to keep an eye on what your children are using. Many children are finding they are areas where they are becoming targets for being bullied. Being bullied can have a traumatic outcome in a child's life.

If you suspect you know someone who is struggling either from being bullied or having suicidal thoughts please reach out and talk to them, sometimes it is a friendly ear they need someone to understand and just be there to listen. Other people may show no signs that they are feeling suicidal and hide their feelings pretending that everything is alright.

Building a support network for the person is always a good idea: family, friends, and support groups are a good place to start. If you feel, someone may be at risk you need more help don't hesitate to ring emergency services in your area. Some may find themselves, after they helped someone through this hard time will feel overwhelmed by their experience, and may need to reach out to someone to talk about what they have been through.

8

My Journey

In this journey, I've discovered that bereavement adjustment is not about avoidance but about acknowledging the full spectrum of emotions—sadness, anger, confusion, and even moments of joy. These feelings coexist, and allowing space for them has been crucial in my healing process. It's a testament to the love we shared, a love that doesn't simply vanish but transforms over time. Rather than trying to suppress my grief, I've learned to embrace it, finding comfort in the memories and experiences that define our relationship.

Listening to the stories of others who have experienced similar losses has been a source of solace and understanding. It's a reminder that we are not alone in our struggles. There is a unique bond, formed among those who have faced such heartache, a shared understanding that transcends words. In these conversations, I have found that there is power in vulnerability. By sharing our stories, we not only honor our loved ones but also create a safe space for others to express their grief without fear of judgment.

As I navigated through my grief, I also discovered the importance of kindness—both to myself and to others. It's easy to fall into a cycle of self-blame and despair, but I've learned that extending grace to myself has been essential. Grief doesn't follow a timeline, and some days are more challenging than others. Acknowledging this has allowed me to be gentler with myself during the rough patches.

Moreover, kindness has a ripple effect. When I allowed myself to experience love and compassion, it inspired me to extend that same kindness to others, who are grieving. Whether it's a simple message of support or being present for a friend in need, these small acts can create meaningful connections. We may never fully understand the depths of an other's pain, but our willingness to listen and share can provide a glimmer of hope.

Another aspect of my journey has been embracing the notion of optimism, not as a denial of sorrow but as a choice to find moments of light an other's darkness. I've learned that it's possible to laugh and feel joy even while carrying the weight of grief. This realization has been liberating; it has allowed me to celebrate my loved one's life rather than solely mourn their loss.

Ultimately, grief is a testament to the love we shared, a love that endures beyond physical presence. It transforms as we move forward, allowing us to carry our loved ones with us in our hearts. The road is long and winding, filled with unexpected twists, but it is a journey worth taking. If you find yourself navigating similar waters, know that healing is possible, and it's okay to seek help along the way. Together, we can shine a light in the darkness and create a tapestry of support, hope, and love.

9

Conclusion

Regarding the healing process following the death of my son, I have learned that coping with death in all its forms is imperative. Accepting sadness, and rage as well as the rare moments of happiness, I chose to see that love is forever.

Grief does not follow a single dimension as it is an intricate web that teaches us to hold our loved ones in their heart. With every hit, I am taken back to that moment communally shared and how that memory has shaped and reconstructed one's understanding of love and loss, more importantly, love post-loss. Besides that, kindness has become an indisputable factor not only towards others but equally important, towards myself.

Such love, forgiveness, and compassion would not only benefit me but will benefit those around me to assist them in coping with their struggles. It makes grief more bearable as and when it is shared. Indifference is extremely justified, for difficulties and will be there, and so are opportunities for great growth, understanding, and hope. In the same manner, let us shine a brighter future ahead by way of converting our pain to love.

10

Resources

The Alliance of Hope for Suicide Loss Survivors. (2024, July 3). Alliance of Hope for Suicide Loss Survivors. https://allianceofhope.org/

Mental Health Foundation. (n.d.). *Home*. https://mentalhealth.org.nz/

Facts about Suicide. (2024, April 25). Suicide Prevention. https://www.cdc.gov/suicide/facts/index.html